Thurgood Marshall

by Helen Frost

Consulting Editor: Gail Saunders-Smith, Ph.D.

Consultant: Kathy Shurtleff, Assistant Director,
Supreme Court Historical Society

Pebble Books

an imprint of Capstone Press
Mankato, Minnesota

Pebble Books are published by Capstone Press
1710 Roe Crest Drive, North Mankato, Minnesota 56003
www.capstonepub.com

Library of Congress Cataloging-in-Publication Data
Frost, Helen, 1949–
  Thurgood Marshall/by Helen Frost.
  p. cm. —(Famous Americans)
  Summary: An introduction to the life and accomplishments of the African
American civil rights attorney who became a prominent Supreme Court Justice.
  Includes bibliographical references and index.
  ISBN-13: 978-0-7368-1643-4 (hardcover)
  ISBN-10: 0-7368-1643-7 (hardcover)
  ISBN-13: 978-0-7368-3377-6 (softcover pbk.)
  ISBN-10: 0-7368-3377-3 (softcover pbk.)
  1. Marshall, Thurgood, 1908–1993—Juvenile literature. 2. United States.
Supreme Court—Biography—Juvenile literature. 3. Judges—United States—
Biography—Juvenile literature. [1. Marshall, Thurgood, 1908–1993. 2. Lawyers.
3. Judges. 4. African Americans—Biography.] I. Marshall, Thurgood, 1908–1993.
II. Title. III. Series.
KF8745.M34 F76 2003
347.73'2634—dc21   2002012233

Note to Parents and Teachers

The Famous Americans series supports national history standards for units on people and culture. This book describes and illustrates the life of Thurgood Marshall. The photographs support early readers in understanding the text. This book also introduces early readers to subject-specific vocabulary words, which are defined in the Words to Know section. Early readers may need assistance in reading some words and to use the Table of Contents, Words to Know, Read More, Internet Sites, and Index/Word List sections of the book.

Table of Contents

4

Thurgood Marshall was born in Maryland on July 2, 1908. His mother was a teacher. His father worked for a railroad company.

view of Maryland in the early 1900s

6

Thurgood's mother taught him that school was important. His father taught him how to argue carefully.

a young Thurgood

8

Segregation was legal when
Thurgood was growing up.
White people and
African American people had
to go to separate schools.

Thurgood finished high school and went to college. After college he studied law at Howard University. Thurgood was the best student in his law class.

Thurgood was married two times. His first wife, Vivian Burey, died in 1955. Then he married Cecilia Suyat. They had two sons.

Thurgood, Cecilia, and their two sons

14

Thurgood became a lawyer. He was very good at his job. Thurgood wanted to change the laws that made people with different skin colors go to different schools.

Thurgood practicing for a case

Thurgood brought a case to the Supreme Court and won. After that, students of different skin colors could go to the same schools.

18

In 1967, President Johnson named Thurgood to be the first African American justice on the U.S. Supreme Court. Thurgood held that job for 24 years.

Thurgood being sworn in as a Supreme Court justice with President Johnson standing at his left side

20

Thurgood died in 1993.
He was 84 years old.
People remember that
Thurgood Marshall helped
make laws fair for everyone.

Words to Know

African American—a citizen of the United States with an African background

argue—to give an opinion about something

case—a matter that comes before a court of law

justice—a judge in a court of law

lawyer—a person who is trained to help people with the law; lawyers represent people who go to court.

legal—allowed by law

segregation—the act or practice of keeping people or groups apart because of their skin color

Supreme Court—the highest and most powerful court in the United States; the Supreme Court has the power to change decisions that are made in lower courts; the Supreme Court has nine justices.

Read More

Adler, David A. *A Picture Book of Thurgood Marshall.* Picture Book Biography. New York: Holiday House, 1997.

Hitzeroth, Deborah, and Sharon Leon. *Thurgood Marshall.* The Importance Of. San Diego: Lucent Books, 1997.

Kent, Deborah. *Thurgood Marshall and the Supreme Court.* Cornerstones of Freedom. New York: Children's Press, 1997.

Internet Sites

Track down many sites about Thurgood Marshall. Visit the FACT HOUND at *http://www.facthound.com*

IT IS EASY! IT IS FUN!

1) Go to *http://www.facthound.com*

2) Type in: 0736816437

3) Click on "FETCH IT" and FACT HOUND will find several links hand-picked by our editors.

Relax and let our pal FACT HOUND do the research for you!

23

Index/Word List

Word Count: 200
Early-Intervention Level: 19

Editorial Credits
Hollie J. Endres, editor; Clay Schotzko/Icon Productions, cover designer;
    Molly Nei, designer; Karrey Tweten, photo researcher

Photo Credits
Corbis, 6, 14; Hulton-Deutsch Collection, 4, 18; Thomas L. Schafer, 8 (top);
    Bettmann, 10, 20
Getty Images/Hulton/CNP/Archive, cover; Hulton Archive, 1, 16
Library of Congress, 12
Schomberg Center/New York Public Library, 8 (bottom)

The author thanks the children's library staff at the Allen County Public Library
in Fort Wayne, Indiana, for research assistance.